A BOOK OF EPITAPHS

A BOOK OF
EPITAPHS

Raymond Lamont-Brown

David & Charles
Newton Abbot London North Pomfret (Vt)

British Library Cataloguing in Publication Data

Lamont-Brown, Raymond
  A book of epitaphs.
  1. Epitaphs — England
  I. Title
  929.5   PN6291

  ISBN 0-7153-8311-6

Typeset by Typesetters (Birmingham) Ltd.,
and printed in Great Britain
by A. Wheaton & Co., Exeter
for David & Charles (Publishers) Limited
Brunel House Newton Abbot Devon

Published in the United States of America
by David & Charles Inc
North Pomfret Vermont 05053 USA

CONTENTS

INTRODUCTION

> Let there be no inscription upon my tomb; let no man write my epitaph: no man can write my epitaph.

Robert Emmet (1780—1803): *Speech on his trial and conviction for high treason*, September 1803

> Of all funerall honours (saith Camden) Epitaphs have always been most respective; for in them love was shewn to the deceased, memorie was continued to posterity, friends were comforted, and the Reader put in minde of Human frailtie.

Weever: *Funerall Monuments*, 1631

This is my seventh anthology of epitaphs and it represents everything that I have found concerning them which is humorous, sad, witty and outrageous. Unlike other forms of doggerel the epitaph presents every aspect of man's emotions from laughter to tears, from courage to cowardice, from confidence to fear, from sentiment to piety, and from irony to wisdom.

Epitaphs remain much more than just monuments to the dead. They are a rich source of social history; they record the continuity of life; they tell us much about the occupations of people who once lived in a particular district; and they mirror the social scene. The epitaph is a much underrated verse form—a complete entity and sometimes a piece of literary genius.

Britain is particularly rich in epitaphs. Many of these are the last remnants of localised folk-lay and ballad; and many are the last relics of fascinating worthies who but for the epitaph would have been long forgotten.

The earliest tombs to be found in parish churches in Britain are those of the twelfth century, marked by simple stone slabs. At that time, burials inside churches were mainly reserved for ecclesiastics and abbots. By the thirteenth century, the recumbent effigy had made its appearance. These tombs, with their simple Latin inscriptions, tell us much about the dress, armour and heraldry of the time. By the fourteenth century, a step further had been taken with the introduction of the richly-carved, stone canopy. The setting up of these early tombs and epitaphs, of which only a few now remain, was a major source of employment for many craftsmen during the Middle Ages.

The main materials used were Purbeck and Frosterley marbles, free-stones, sandstone, chalk and Beer-stone, alabaster, wood, latten and bronze. Much of the original decoration and gilt work has now gone.

The epitaphs of medieval times were usually in the form of tender prayers, whereas those of Eliza-bethan and Jacobean ages more often provide a historical record describing who a person was and what he did. From 1600 to the Civil War, epitaphs were poetic, changing to brief inscriptions under the Commonwealth, and back to long-winded effusions from 1660 to 1680. Many epitaphs are of a humorous, even irreligious nature. Such levity in the churchyard may seem strange to us now, but the use of churchyards for sport, markets and pleasure was an old-established and persistent custom. There are records as early as the fourth century of St Basil protesting against the holding of markets in church-yards on the pretext of making preparations for festivals. But, even though such dignitaries as the canons of the Synod of Exeter of 1287 strictly asked their parish priests to make sure that 'combats, dances, or other improper sports . . . or stage plays or farces' *(ludos theatrales et ludebriorum spectacula)* were prohibited, the fairs persisted and often ale was brewed on the church premises.

It is not a platitude to say that graveyards are the richest source of epitaphs, for epitaphs seem to crop up in the most unlikely places. Sometimes epitaphs got no further than the writing of them, and perhaps that said to have been written of Frederick, Prince of Wales, by his father King George II, is the one most full of an unnatural hatred. 'I have lost my eldest son,' the monarch proclaimed, 'and I am glad.'

While all the epitaphs herein are authentic and genuine, in that they once embellished the tombs of the deceased (or were devised with that in mind), it should be noted that as time passes they become less and less accessible. Church renovation, weather, vandalism and many other reasons may have caused some of the epitaphs to be moved from their original settings, thus a collector should not be surprised nor disappointed if a few are not to be found any longer.

St Andrews
November 1981

CHURCHYARD HUMOUR

Here lie the bones of Elizabeth Charlotte,
Born a virgin, died a harlot.
She was aye a virgin at seventeen,
A remarkable thing in Aberdeen.

JOHN SIM OF PETERHEAD

Wha lies here?
John Sim, ye needna' speir.
Hullo, John, is that you?
Ay, ay, but I'm deed noo.

TO ROSE HERRING (Whitby, North Yorkshire)

The freshest of all Herrings once was this,
Sweet as the new-born Rose.
In hope of awakening to eternal bliss,
Now in foul pickle she does here repose.

IN FORFAR CHURCHYARD

'Tis here that Tibby Allan lies,
'Tis here, or here about,
But no one till the Resurrection day,
Shall the very spot dispute.

A BEDFORDSHIRE WORTHY (Luton Parish Church)

Here lies the body of THOMAS PROCTER,
Who lived and died without a doctor.

IN CULLEN GRAVEYARD, BANFFSHIRE

Here lies interred a man o'micht,
His name was Malcome Downie:
He lost his life ae market nicht
By fa'in aff his pownie.
                    Aged 37 years.

9

To a drunken fiddler who drowned in the Lough (the memorial tablet is in the shape of a violin)

August ye 15 1770

Beware ye fidlers of ye fidlers fate
Nor tempt ye deep least ye repeant to late
Ye ever have been deemed to water foes
Then shun ye lake till it with whiskey floes
On firm land only exercise your skill
There you may play and drink your fill.

UNLUCKY MR LAMB FROM HUNTINGDON

On the 29th November
A confounded piece of timber
Came down, bang slam
And killed I, John Lamb.

AN IRISHMAN'S COMMENT (Belturbet churchyard, County Cavan)

Here lies JOHN HIGLEY, whose father and mother were drowned on their passage from America. Had both lived, they would have been buried here.

FROM ST ANDREW'S CHURCHYARD, CAMBRIDGE

Man's life is like a winter's day:
Some only breakfast and away:
Others to dinner stay, and are well fed:
The oldest man but sups, and goes to bed:
Long is his life who lingers out the day,
Who goes the soonest has the least to pay.

THE MISER'S TOMB (Dorchester Abbey, Oxfordshire)

Here lieth one who for medicine would not give
A little gold: and so his life was lost.
I fancy that he'd wish again to live
Did he know how much his funeral cost.

JUST ENOUGH

Poems and epitaphs are but stuff:
Here lies ROBERT BURROWS, that's enough.

THE WISH OF THE LIVING (St Agnes' churchyard, Cornwall)

Here lies the body of Joan Carthew,
Born at St Columb; died at St Cue:
Children she had five,
Three dead and two alive:
Those that are dead choosing rather
To die with their mother than live with their father.

FROM A LOVING WIFE (Wrexham churchyard)

RICHARD KENDRICK
Was buried August 29th, 1785,
By the desire of his wife,
MARGARET KENDRICK

A DISMAL STORY (Pentewan, Cornwall)

In this here grave ye see before ye,
Lies buried up a dismal story;
A young maiden she wor crossed in love,
And tooken to the realms above.
But he that crossed her I should say,
Deserves to go t'other way.

IT'S ALL THE SAME! (Kingsbridge, Devon)

Here I lie, at the chancel door,
Here I lie, because I'm poor:
The farther in the more you pay,
Here I lie as warm as they.

MR DAY FROM POOLE

As long as can be,
So long so long was he;
How long, how long, dost say?
As long as the longest DAY.

ROBERT TROLLOPE OF GATESHEAD

Here lies ROBERT TROLLOPE,
Who made your stones roll up.
When Death took his soul up,
His body fill'd this hole up.

11

LINES ON A STUBBORN HUSBAND (Dun Dealgan, County Louth)

Here lies the body of Robert Moore.
What signifies more words?
He killed himself by eating curds.
But if he'd been ruled by Sarah, his wife,
He might have lived out all the days of his life.

THE TALL MAN FROM DUMFRIES

Here lies Andrew MacPherson,
Who was a peculiar person;
He stood six foot two
Without his shoe,
And he was slew,
At Waterloo.

OF JOHN HILL OF MANCHESTER

Here lies JOHN HILL
A man of skill
His age was five times ten;
He ne'er did good,
Nor ever would,
Had he lived as long again.

FROM A WESLEYAN CHAPEL, BOLTON

Her manners mild, her temper such
Her language good, and not too much.

THE LIGHTNING CONDUCTOR (Great Torrington, Devon)

Here lies a man who was killed by lightning;
He died when his prospects seemed to be
   brightening.
He might have cut a flash in this world of trouble,
But the flash cut him, and he lies in the stubble.

MARYPORT'S CELESTIAL TRAVELLER

Ann Brown left Maryport and started for Paradise
                              25 June 1801.

Reader, of these four lines take heed,
And mend your life for my sake.
For you must die, like Archie Reed,
Tho' you read till your eyes ache.

MARY WAS BOSS! (Chelmsford, Essex)

Here lies the man Richard,
And Mary his wife
Whose surname was Prichard
They lived without strife
And the reason was plain
They abounded in riches
They had no care nor pain
And his wife wore the breeches.

AN AUNTIE (Crail, Fife)

Here lies my good and gracious Auntie,
Wham death has packed in his portmanty,
Three score and ten years God did gift her,
And here she lies, wha de'il daurs lift her?

FROM PAINSWICK CHURCHYARD, GLOUCESTERSHIRE

My wife lies dead, and here she lies,
Nobody laughs and nobody cries:
Where she is gone to and how she fares,
Nobody knows and nobody cares.

FROM A CORNISH CHURCHYARD

Here lies two babbies, dead as nits,
Who died while eating cherry bits,
They were too good to live with we,
So God did take to live with He.

ANGELINE OF LARKHILL, WILTSHIRE

1790

Now Angeline was a harlot bold
Who's sleeping here in the frost and cold.
Stop, passer by! If you are willing.
She was never known to refuse a shilling.

(Hereford churchyard)

An enormous number of epitaphs were written by husbands about their wives, suggesting that at last they had the last word. Here at Hereford a wife wrote this about herself, addressed to her husband:

> Grieve not for me, my husband dear,
> I am not dead but sleeping here,
> With patience wait, prepare to die,
> And in short time you'll come to I.

The husband, having received a legacy from his late wife, carved this reply below:

> I am not grieved, my dearest wife,
> Sleep on I've got another wife.
> Therefore I cannot come to thee,
> For I'm going to spend the cash on she.

FROM ST ALBAN'S CATHEDRAL BURIAL GROUND

> Sacred to the memory of Martha Gwynn,
> Who was so very pure within,
> She burst the outer shell of sin,
> And hatched herself a cherubim.

THE GLUTTON OF SKYE

> Here lie the bones,
> O Tonald Jones,
> The wale o'men
> For eating scones.
> Eating scones
> And drinking yill,
> Till his last moans
> He took his fill.

IN GRANTHAM CHURCHYARD, LINCOLNSHIRE

> John Palfreyman, who lyeth here,
> Was aged four and twenty year:
> And near this place his mother lies,
> Also his father, when he dies.

ALONE AT LAST

> Here snug in her grave my wife doth lie,
> Now she's at rest and so am I.

14

THERE WAS AN OLD LADY (Ryde churchyard, Isle of Wight)

> There was an old lady from Ryde
> Who ate some apples and dyed.
> The apples fermented inside the lamented
> Made cider inside her inside.

FROM A CHURCHYARD IN LIVERPOOL

> Poor John lies buried here:
> Although he was both hale and stout,
> Death stretched him on the bitter bier,
> In another world he hops about.

John was a barman!

FROM ST HILDA'S, HARTLEPOOL

> Ephraim Judd : The Card Maker

His card is cut: Long days he shuffled through
The game of life: he dealt as others do.
Though he by honours tells not its amount
When the last trump is play'd, his tricks will count.

A SENSIBLE MAN (Newtyle churchyard, Ruthven, Perthshire)

> Here lies the body of Robert Small,
> Who, when in life, was thick not tall;
> But what's of greater consequence,
> He was endowed with good sense.

OBIT 1690

> Here lies the bones,
> Of JOSEPH JONES
> Who ate whilst he was able:
> But, once o'erfed,
> He dropped down dead,
> And fell beneath the table.
> When from this tomb,
> To meet his doom
> He rises amidst sinners;
> Since he must dwell
> In Heaven or Hell,
> To take him, which gives best dinners.

FROM FROME CHURCHYARD

Reader, Death took me without any warning,
I was well at night and died in the morning.

A MOTHER (Wolstanton, Staffordshire)

Some have children, some have none:
Here lies the mother of twenty-one.

THE GRAVE OF THE TWO WIVES OF TOM SEXTON

Here lies the body of Sarah Sexton,
She was a wife that never vexed one;
I can't say as much for the one at the next stone.

IN AN ESSEX COUNTRY CHURCHYARD

Underneath this tuft doth lie
Back to back my wife and I.
Generous stranger, spare a tear,
For could she speak, I cannot hear.
Happier far than when in life,
Free from noise and free from strife.
When the last trump the air doth fill,
If she gets up then I'll lie still.

MR MILES OF ESHER

This tombstone is a Milestone:
Ha! How so?
Because beneath lies MILES, who's
Miles below.

ANOTHER MILES

The smallest grave in Huntingdonshire
The grave of Miles Button
Miles in length, Miles in breadth, Miles in depth,
and after all is only a button-hole!

FROM SUTTON BINGHAM CHURCHYARD, SOMERSET

Here lies my poor wife,
Without bed or blanket,
But dead as a door-nail,
The Lord be thanked.

IN DURNESS CHURCHYARD, SUTHERLAND

> Here doth lye the bodie
> Of John Flye, who did die
> By a stroke from a sky-rocket,
> Which hit him in the eye-socket.

FROM ST MICHAEL'S CHURCHYARD, DUMFRIES

> Here lyes Bedal Willy Smyth,
> Wha rang the auld kirk bell,
> He buryed thousands in his day,
> And here he lies himsel'.
> Some say he was a marriyed man,
> Some say he was no,
> But iv he ever had a spouse,
> She's no wi' him below.

TEAGUE O'BRIEN (Ballyhareen churchyard, County Tipperary)

> Here I at length repose,
> My spirit now at aise is,
> With the tips of my toes
> And the point of my nose,
> Turned up to the roots of the daisies.

THE WIFE OF JOHN FORD (Potterne churchyard, Wiltshire)

> Here lies Mary, the wife of John Ford,
> We hope her soul is gone to the Lord;
> But if for Hell she has chang'd this life
> She had better be there than be John Ford's wife.

THE WOODMAN OF OAKHAM

> The Lord saw good, I was lopping off wood,
> And down fell from the tree,
> I met with a check and broke my neck,
> And so death lopped off me.

JOLLITY (Leeds Parish Church, West Yorkshire)

> Here lies my wife,
> Here lies she;
> Hallelujah!
> Hallelujee!

DEAN CHURCHYARD, BOLTON

> A ponderous load on me did fall,
> And killed me dead against this wall.

THE CATTLE DEALER (Kirkmichael, Perthshire)

> Here lies the body of Glencorse,
> He went to the borders with two horse,
> He was a sheep and cattle-dealer
> At last gave up for want of siller.

TREAD SILENTLY (Troutbeck, Cumbria)

> Here lies a woman, no man can deny it,
> She died in peace, although she lived unquiet;
> Her husband prays, if e'er this way you walk,
> You would tread softly — if she wake she'll talk.

AMERICAN EPILAUGHS

> Here lies the body of JEEMS HUMBRICK
> who was accidentally shot
> on the banks of the Pacus river
> by a young man.

He was accidentally shot with one of the large Colt's revolver with no stopper for the cock on it was of the old fashioned kind brass mounted and of such is the Kingdom of Heaven.

FROM ROCKVILLE, MASSACHUSETTS

> In memory of JANE BENT
> Who kick'd her heels and away she went.

NEW JERSEY SENTIMENT

> Reader, pass on, don't waste your time
> On bad biography, and bitter rhyme:
> For what I am, this crumbling clay insures,
> And what I was is no affair of yours.

AND FROM THE SAME STATE

> JULIA ADAMS
> Died through wearing thin shoes
> April 17th 1839
> Aged 19 years.

JEFFREY HAZARD (Peacedale, Narrangansett, Rhode Island)
He was called 'Stout Jeffrey' because of his strength.

> Stout Jeffrey Hazard lifted this stone
> In pounds just sixteen twenty one,
> In South Kingston he lived and died,
> God save us all from sinful pride.

MASSACHUSETTS MEDITATIONS

I came in the morning — it was Spring,
          And I smiled;
I walk'd out at noon — it was Summer,
          And I was glad;
I sat me down at even — it was Autumn,
          And I was sad;
I laid me down at night — it was Winter,
          And I slept.

PHILADELPHIA PEOPLE

In memory of HENRY WANG, son of his Father and
Mother, John and Maria Wang. Died Dec. 31st,
1829, aged 1—2 hour.

          A short-lived joy
          Was our little boy.
          He has gone on high,
          So don't you cry.

PENNSYLVANIA WARNING

Eliza, sorrowing, rears this marble slab
To her dear JOHN, who died of eating crab.

FROM THE CHURCHYARD, SARATOGA SPRINGS

Farewell, dear wife! my life is past;
I loved you while my life did last;
Don't grieve for me, or sorrow take,
But love my brother for my sake.

FROM BURLINGTON CHURCHYARD, IOWA

Beneath this stone our baby lays
He neither cries nor hollers
He lived just one and twenty days,
And cost us forty dollars.

FROM LICHFIELD, CONNECTICUT

Sacred to the memory of inestimable worth, of
unrivalled excellence and virtue — —, whose
ethereal parts became seraphic on the 25th day of
May, 1867.

IN BURLINGTON CHURCHYARD, MASSACHUSETTS

Sacred to the memory of Anthony Drake,
Who died for peace and quietness sake;
His wife was constantly scolding and scoffin',
So he sought for repose in a twelve-dollar coffin.

FROM NEW JERSEY

She was not smart, she was not fair,
But hearts with grief for her are swellin';
And empty stands her little chair:
She died of eatin' water melon.

FROM A CHURCHYARD IN CONNECTICUT

Here lies, cut down like unripe fruit,
The wife of Deacon Amos Shute:
She died of drinking too much coffee,
Anny Dominy eighteen forty.

FROM THE WESLEYAN CEMETERY, ST LOUIS

Here lize a stranger braiv,
Who died while fightin' the Suthern Confederacy to
   save
Piece to his dust.
Brave Suthern friend
From island 10.

You reached a Glory us end.
We plase these flowrs above the stranger's hed,
In honour of the shiverlus ded.
Sweet spirit rest in Heven
Ther'l be know yankis there.

SOLOMON PEASE OF SEARSPORT, MAINE

Under the sod, and under the trees,
Here lies the body of Solomon Pease.
The Pease are not here, there's only the Pod —
The Pease shelled out and went to God.

THE BAKER FROM RUIDOSO, NEW MEXICO

Here lies John Yeast
Pardon me for not rising.

FROM CHERAW CHURCHYARD, SOUTH CAROLINA

> My name, my country,
> What are they to thee?
> What, whether high or low,
>   My pedigree?
> Perhaps I far surpassed
>   All other men:
> Perhaps I fall below them all;
>   What then?
> Suffice it, stranger,
> Thou see'st a tomb,
> Thou know'st its use;
> It hides — no matter whom.

ON A JUDGE'S GRAVE, LOUISIANA

'Call silence!' the Judge to the officer cries;
'This hubbub and talk, will it never be done?
Those people this morning have made such a noise,
We've decided ten cases without hearing one.'

FROM VIRGINIA

> To this church I once went,
> But I grieved and I sorrowed;
> For the season was Lent
> And the sermon was borrowed.

CONNECTICUT ACCOUNTANCY

At length my friends the feast of life is o'er;
I've eat sufficient — and I'll drink no more;
My night is come; I've spent a jovial day;
'Tis time to part; but oh! — what is to pay?

FROM AUGUSTA, MAINE

> Our little Jacob
> Has been taken from this earthly garden
> To bloom in a superior flower-pot
>   Above.

FROM LEE COUNTY, MISSISSIPPI

> Once I Wasn't
> Then I Was
> Now I ain't again.

From the Forgotten Graves of Goldminers
(Desolation Canyon, Death Valley, California)

MARTHA MAYS OF THE GOLD NUGGET SALOON

Here lies the body of Martha Mays
Who was so virginal in stays,
She lived to the age of three score and ten
And gave to the worms what she refused to the men.

YOUNG ABE LOUTH

Here lies the body of Young Abe Louth
Who died of an ornery wisdom tooth.

ON WHISKY JOE

He had some faults
And many merits
He died of drinking
Home brewed spirits.

ANDY MONNEY'S WIFE

Here lies my poor wife,
A bitch and a shrew
If I said I missed her
I should lie too.

HANNAH'S THREE IN A ROW

This old rock has drunk a widow's tear
Three of my husbands are buried here.

COOKHOUSE JAKE

Peace to his hashes.

JOHN SMITH, OF SANTA DIGGINGS

In memory of John Smith, who met Wierlent
    Death near this ole spot
18 hundert and 40 too. He was shot with his own .42
It warrn't one o'them noo fangl't kind
But one o'them with brass knobs and an ole kind
    o'barrel.
    Such is the Kingdom of Heaven.

PETE CONNOR, OF HIS WIFE NANCY

Who far below in this grave doth rest
She's join'd the army of the blest;
The Lord has ta'en her to the sky,
The saints rejoice, and so do I.

FAT MAY PRESTON

Here lies the body of
Fat May Preston
Who's now moved to heaven
To relieve the congestion.

UNLUCKY BILL SMEE

Here lies Wild Bill Smee
Who ran for sheriff in '83
He also ran in '84
But ain't a runnin' any more!

CHARLOTTE THE HARLOT OF COPPERSTONE CREEK

Here lies the bones of Copperstone Charlotte
Once a schoolmarm, then a harlot
For sixteen whole years she kep' her virginity
A darn'd long time in this vicinity.

APPLY WITHIN

Here lies the body of Henry Oakes, gunslinger.
If not, notify Chantry & Son, Undertakers, at once.

RHYMIN' PETE

Living and dying I loved the truth
And I'll speak it now, though it seem uncouth;
I wrote thirty poems, and was published as well,
So I don't care now if it's Heaven or Hell!

LARRY THE LUSH

Here lie the earthly remains of
Larry G. Chappell
He hath joined the spirits
Of which he was always so fond.

Restin'.

PERCY THE PRETTY BOY

The mortal remains of Percy Claud Crintle
Lie in the dust under this old lintle.
He worked with us all without any shame
And all he had left was his pretty name.

AND AN AMERICAN MISCELLANY

Here does the body of MARY ANNE REST,
With her head on Abraham's breast.
It's a very good thing for Mary Anne,
But it's very hard lines on Abraham.

A much esteemed but injudicious man,
Caught a cold in Jan.
He tangled thus in fate's mysterious web,
He died in Feb.

Here lie the remains of poor CHRISTOPHER TYPE,
The rest of him couldn't be found:
He sat on a powder keg, smoking a pipe,
While the wind blew the ashes around.

He scraped away the mossy spray
And scratched amid the lichen green,
Until he read: 'Kate Kelly, dead,
Aged twenty-seven. Kerosene.'

He turned the corner with a moan,
By thirst for knowledge goaded
And found another stone:
Didn't know 'twas loaded.'

JUST FOR THE FAMOUS

WILLIAM SHAKESPEARE, d 1616 (Church of the Holy Trinity, Stratford-upon-Avon)

> Good friend, for Jesu's sake forbeare
> To digg the dust enclosed here;
> Blessed by ye man yt spares these stones,
> And curst be he yt moves my bones.

ETHELBURGA, QUEEN OF THE WEST SAXONS, DIED *c* AD 617

I was, I am not; smil'd, that since did weep,
Labour'd, short rest, I walk'd that now must sleep:
I play'd, I play not; sung, that now am still;
Saw, that am blind; I would, that have no will;
I fed that, which feeds worms; I stood, I fell,
I bade God save you, that now bid farewell.
I felt, I feel not; follow'd, was pursued;
I would, have peace; I conquer'd, am subdu'd;
I moved, want motion; I was stiff that bow
Below the earth; then something, nothing now.
I catch'd, am caught. I travelled, here I lie;
Liv'd in the World, that to the World now die.

DR JOHN POTTER, ARCHBISHOP OF CANTERBURY, d 1736

> Alack and well a-day
> Potter himself is turned to clay.

DAVID HUME, SCOTTISH PHILOSOPHER, d 1776 (Calton Hill, Edinburgh)

> Within this circular idea,
> Call'd vulgarly a tomb,
> The ideas and impressions lie,
> That constituted Hume.

MRS OLDFIELD, ACTRESS, d 1730

> This we must own in justice to her shade,
> 'Tis the first bad exit OLDFIELD ever made.

Hail, warlike Alfred, high and noble birth,
Give labour to thine honour, honour to thy worth
Labour procured renown, but joys with grief
Are ever blended; to fear hope brings relief:
Today of Victor, tomorrow sees thee armed,
The foe though Victor, finds thee still unharmed;
Reeking with sweat thy garb, thy sword with gore,
Prove what a weight you felt the regal power.
No one but thee, through the wild world's domain
Under such toils could rise and breathe again:
Thy sword, though blunted by such bloody strife,
Thou didst not sheathe, nor by it end thy life —
But after many a struggle for thy throne,
Thou found'st peace and life in Christ alone.

SIR JOHN STRANGE, d 1754

Here lies an honest lawyer —
That is Strange!

CHARLES AND MARY LAMB (All Saints' churchyard,
Edmonton, North London)

Charles was the noted English essayist.

To the Memory of
CHARLES LAMB,
Died 27th Decr. 1834, aged 59.
Farewell dear friend, that smile, that harmless
mirth
No more shall gladden our domestic hearth;
That rising tear, that pain forbid to flow,
Better than words no more assuage our woe;
That hand outstretched, from small but well earned
store,
Yield succour to the destitute no more
Yet art thou not all lost; thro' many an age
With sterling sense and humour shall thy page
Win many an English bosom, pleased to see
That old and happier vein revived in thee.
This for our earth, and if with friends we share
Our joys in Heaven, *we hope* to meet thee there.
Also MARY ANNE LAMB
sister of the above,
Born 3rd Decr 1767, died 20th May 1847.

He wrote his own epitaph.

The Body of
B. FRANKLIN
Printer
Like the cover of an old book,
its contents torn out,
and stripped of its lettering and gilding,
lies here, food for worms.
But the work shall not be wholly lost;
for it will, as he believed, appear once more,
in a new and more perfect condition,
corrected and amended
by the Author.

ROBIN HOOD, LEGENDARY OUTLAW AND HERO, d 1247
(Kirklees, near Mirfield, West Yorkshire)

> Hear undernead this latil stean
> Laiz Robert Earl of Huntingdon,
> Nea arcir ver az hie sa geud,
> An pipil kauld him Robin Heud.
> Sich atlaz az he an iz men
> Vil England nior si again.

BEN JONSON, ENGLISH POET AND DRAMATIST, d 1637

Written by lyric poet Robert Herrick.

> Here lies Jonson with the rest
> Of the poets, but the best.
> Reader, would'st thou more have known?
> Ask his story, not the stone;
> That will speak what this can't tell
> Of his glory; so farewell!

ANNE OF DENMARK, WIFE OF JAMES I & VI, d 1619

Marche with his winde hath strucke a cedar tall
And weeping April mournes the cedar's fall.
And May intends no flowers her month shall bring,
Since she must lose the flower of all the spring.
Thus Marche's winde hath caused April showers
And yet sad May must loose her flower of flowers.

DANIEL DEFOE, ENGLISH POLITICAL WRITER (buried in
Bunhill Fields, London)

DANIEL DE-FOE
Born 1661
Died 1731.
Author of
'Robinson Crusoe',
This monument is the result of an appeal
in the 'Christian World' newspaper
to the boys and girls of England for funds
to place a suitable memorial upon the grave
of
DANIEL DE-FOE.
It represents the united contributions
of seventeen hundred persons
Septr 1870.

And to his 'inspiration' Alexander Selkirk, buried
in the churchyard of the Island of Juan Fernandez:

In memory of
ALEXANDER SELKIRK
Mariner.
A native of Largo, in the county of Fife, Scotland.
Who lived on this island, in complete
solitude, for four years, and four months.
He was landed from the 'Cinque Ports' galley,
96 tons, 18 guns, A.D. 1704, and
was taken off in the 'Duke',
privateer, 12th February, 1709.
He died Lieutenant of H.M.S. 'Weymouth',
A.D. 1723, aged 47.
This tablet is erected near Selkirk's lookout
By Commodore Powell and the officers
of H.M.S. 'Topaze', A.D. 1868.

THEODORE, KING OF CORSICA (St Anne's churchyard,
Soho)

Erected in 1758 by Walpole, Earl of Orford.

Near this place is interred
THEODORE, KING OF CORSICA
Who died in this parish
December XI, MDCCLVI.,
Immediately after leaving
The King's Bench Prison,

By the benefit of the Act of Insolvency;
In consequence of which
He registered his Kingdom of Corsica
For the use of his creditors.
The grave — great teacher — to the level brings
Heroes and beggars, galley-slaves and kings.

EARL LLOYD GEORGE OF DWYFOR, BRITISH PRIME
MINISTER, d 1945

He wrote this for himself.

Count not my broken pledges as a crime,
I MEANT them, HOW, I meant them at the time.

WILLIAM HUNTINGDON, d 1813 (buried at the Chapel,
Lewes)

The epitaph of the famous 'Coalheaver Preacher'

Here lies the Coalheaver,
Belov'd of his God, but abhorred of Men.
The Omniscient Judge at the Grand Assize,
Shall ratify and confirm this
To the confusion of the many thousands;
For England and its Metropolis shall know
That there hath been a prophet among them.
                    W.H. S.S. [Sinner Saved]

SAMUEL TAYLOR COLERIDGE, ENGLISH POET AND
CRITIC, d 1834

He penned his own epitaph.

Stop, Christian passer-by! — Stop, child of God.

WILLIAM   HOGARTH,   ENGLISH   ENGRAVER   AND
PAINTER, d 1764 (Chiswick churchyard)

Written by David Garrick.

Farewell, great painter of mankind,
Who reached the noblest point of art;
Whose pictur'd morals charm the mind,
And, thro' the eye, correct the heart.
If genius fire thee, reader stay:
If nature touch thee, drop a tear;
If neither move thee, turn away,
For HOGARTH's honour'd dust lies here.

31

HENDRICK WILLEM VAN LOON, DUTCH-AMERICAN HISTORIAN, d 1944

Here lies
HENDRICK WILLEM VAN LOON
Oh wanderer, if my wish could come true
Then you would be I, and I would be you.

ALEXANDER THE GREAT, d 323 BC

sufficit huic tumulus cui non sufficeret orbis.

(Here a mound suffices for one for whom the world was not large enough.)

DAVID GARRICK, ENGLISH ACTOR AND THEATRICAL MANAGER, d 1779

To paint fair nature, by divine command —
Her magic pencil in his glowing hand —
A Shakespeare rose — then to expand his fame
Wide o'er this 'breathing world', a Garrick came.
Though sunk in death the forms the poet drew,
The actor's genius made them breathe anew;
Though, like the Bard himself, in night they lay,
Immortal Garrick call'd them back today;
And, till Eternity, with power sublime,
Shall mark the mortal hour of hoary Time,
Shakespeare and Garrick like a twin star shall shine.

GUSTAVE FLAUBERT, FRENCH NOVELIST, d 1880

Une fois je pense: 'Il faut que je vive.'
Mais maintenant, je dit: 'Je n'en vois pas la
  nécessité.'

(Once I thought: 'I must live.'
But now, I say: I don't see the need.')

DIFFERING SLANTS

Two British lawyers had a slightly different attitude to epitaph writing. Lord Brougham (1778—1868), one of the chief legal luminaries of the nineteenth century (who had made a great name by defending Queen Caroline against George IV), wished to be remembered for his erudite spoken words:

Here reader, turn your weeping eyes,
My fate a useful moral teaches;
The hole in which my body lies
Would not contain one half my speeches.

Lord Norbury (d 1831), on the other hand, wanted to be a learned legal wit to the end:

He's dead! alas, facetious *punster*,
Whose jokes made learned wigs with fun stir;
From heaven's high court, a tipstaff sent,
To call him to his *pun*-ishment:
Stand to your ropes! ye sextons, ring!
Let all your clappers, ding, dong, ding!
Nor-bury him without his due,
He was himself a Toler too.

The pun in the last line refers to the fact that Toler was Lord Norbury's family name.

MY LORD OF ROCHESTER'S EPITAPH

This epitaph was written for King Charles II by the wit John Wilmot, second Earl of Rochester, at the King's own invitation.

Here lies our Sovereign Lord the King,
Whose word no man relies on;
Who never said a foolish thing,
And never did a wise one.

To which the king replied: 'The matter is easily accounted for: my words were my own, my actions were my ministers.'

JOHN DONNE, CLERGYMAN, RELIGIOUS WRITER, POET, d 1631

Reader, I am to let thee know,
Donne's body only lies below;
For could the grave his soul comprise,
Earth would be richer than the skies

SIR CHRISTOPHER WREN, ARCHITECT, d 1723 (St Paul's Cathedral)

Si monumentum requiris, circumspice.
(If you seek his monument, look around you).

Here Lockyer lies interr'd; enough his name
Speakes, which hath few competitors in fame.
A name, soe great, soe generalle, may scorne
Inscriptions which doe vulgar tombs adorne.
A diminution 'tis, to write in verse
His eulogies, which most men's mouths rehearse.
His virtues and his PILLS are so well knowne
That envy can't confine them under stone,
But they'll survive his dust, and not expire
Till all things else at th' universal fire.
This verse is lost, his PILLS embalm him safe
To future times, without an epitaph.

THE CELEBRATED HIGHWAYMAN (Covent Garden churchyard)

The grave epitaph of the celebrated Claude du Val,
hanged at Tyburn, 1670.

> Here lies Du Val! Reader, if male thou art
> Look to thy purse; if female to thy heart.
> Much havick hath he made of both; for all
> Men he may stand, and women he may fall.

A FEMALE SERJEANT-MAJOR

Wilhelmina Middlehampton of His Majesty's 1st
Foot; who died 13 November, 1834, aged 48.

> A wife and mother, comrade, friend sincere,
> A British soldier brave, lies buried here.
> In Spain and Flushing, and at Waterloo,
> She fought to guard her country from the foe;
> Her comrades, Britons, who survive her, say,
> She acted nobly on that glorious day.

SIR THOMAS WOODCOCK, LORD MAYOR OF LONDON, d 1405

> Hic Jacet, Tom Shorthose,
> Sine tomb, sine sheets, sine riches,
> Ni vixit sine gown,
> Sine cloak, sine shirt, sine breeches.

(*Hic jacet*, here lies: *sine*, without)

A JESTER'S EPITAPH

Here lies the Earl of Suffolk's fool,
Men called him DICKY PEARCE:
His folly served to make folks laugh,
When wit and mirth were scarce.
Poor Dick, alas! is dead and gone —
What signifies the cry!
Dickys enough are still behind,
To laugh at by and by.

THE LADY PUGILIST (Hanslope churchyard, Buckinghamshire)

Strong and athletic was my frame
Far away from home I came
And manly fought with Simon Byrnne
Alas! but lived not to return.

Reader, take warning by my fate
Unless you rue your case too late;
And if you ever fought before
Determine now to fight no more.

SAMUEL FOOTE d 1777 (Westminster Abbey)

Here lies one Foote, whose death may thousands
   save,
For death has now one foot within the grave.

AN AGED RECORD BREAKER (Westminster Abbey)

Thomas Parr of the County of Salop
Born *anno* 1483.
   He lived in the Reigns of Ten princes, viz:—
   Edward the 4th, Edward the 5th,
   Richard the 3rd, Henry the 7th,
   Henry the 8th, Edward the 6th,
   Mary, Elizabeth, James and Charles.
           He died in London,
            Aged 152 years,
And was buried here, November 13th, 1635.

FROM SWEETHEART ABBEY, DUMFRIESSHIRE

Composed by Hugh de Burgh, Prior of Lanercost,
on Devorgilla — widow of John Baliol and mother of
the puppet King John of Scotland — who died in
1289.

In Devorvilla moritur sensata Sibilla,
Cum Marthaque pia, contemplativa Maria;
Da Devorvillam requie, Rex summe potiri
Quam tegit iste lapis cor pariterque viri.

(In Devorgilla, a sybil sage doth die, as
Mary contemplative, as Martha pious;
To her, Oh! deign, high King, rest to impart
Whom this stone covers with her husband's heart.)

MEMORIAL TO SIR RICHARD WORME (Peterborough
Cathedral)

Does Worm eat Worme? Knight Worme this truth
   confirms,
From here, with worms, lies Worme, a dish for
   worms.
Does worm eat Worme? Sure Worme will this deny,
For Worme with worms, a dish for worms don't lie.
'Tis so and 'tis not so, for free from worms,
'Tis certain Worme is blest without his worms.

On one of his many visits to Brighton, King George IV met a remarkable woman, Phoebe Hessel, and asked her how she supported herself in her old age. The old lady replied that she lived mostly on charity. 'Half a guinea a week', she said, 'will make me as happy as a princess.' His Majesty ordered that she be paid that amount out of his allowances until she died.

Even in extreme old age she 'told capital stories, had an excellent memory, and was in every respect most agreeable company'.

In Memory of Phoebe Hessel, who was born at
  Stepney,
1713.
She served for many years as a private soldier
In the 5th Regiment of Foot, in different parts
Of Europe and in the Year 1745 fought under the
Command of the Duke of Cumberland at the Battle
Of Fontenoy where she received a bayonet wound
In her arm.
Her long life which commenced in the time of
Queen Anne extended to the reign of George IV,
By whose munificence she received comfort and
Support in her latter years.
She died at Brighton where she had long resided.
December 12th, 1821. Aged 108 years.

THE FORGOTTEN KING (Wimbledon churchyard, Greater London)

Here is to be found the epitaph of John Martin, natural son of Don John Emmanuel (King of Portugal). To be out of the way, John Martin was sent to England, where he became a gardener.

Though skilful and experienced,
He was modest and unassuming;
And tho' faithful to his masters,
And with reason esteemed,
He was kind to his fellow-servants,
And was therefore beloved.
His family and neighbours lamented his death,
As he was a careful husband, a tender father, and an
  honest man.
    He died March 30th, 1760, aged 66.

The grave of John Metcalf, 'Blind Jack' of Knaresborough, who lost his sight at the age of six after an attack of smallpox. Undaunted, he pursued a normal life, married, became a soldier and was present on the bloody field of Culloden (1746). After his army career, in 1754 he was the first to set up a stage-waggon service between York and Knaresborough, and his uncanny judgement led him to take on roadmaking. When he died in 1801 he had the making of bridges, houses and hundreds of miles of roads in Yorkshire, Lancashire, Cheshire and Derbyshire to his credit.

Obit 26th April, 1801. Aged 93.

Here lies JOHN METCALF, one whose infant sight
Felt the dark pressure of an endless night;
Yet such the fervour of his dauntless mind,
His limbs full strung, his spirit unconfined,
That, long ere yet life's bolder years began;
The sightless efforts marked th'aspiring man
Nor marked in vain — high deeds his manhood
  dared,
And commerce, travel, both his ardour shared.
'Twas his a guide's unerring aid to lend —
O'er trackless wastes to bid new roads extend;
And, when rebellion reared her giant size,
'Twas his to burn with patriot enterprise;
For parting wife and babes, a pang to feel,
Then welcome danger for his country's weal.
Reader, like him, exert thy utmost talent given!
Reader, like him, adore the bounteous hand of
  Heaven.

NEAR ROB ROY'S GRAVE, BALQUHIDDER, PERTHSHIRE

Beneath this stane lies Shanet Roy,
Shon Roy's reputed mother;
In all her life this Shon Roy
She never had another.

'Tis here or hereabouts, they say,
The place no one can tell;
But when she'll rise at the last day,
She'll ken the stane hersel'.

OF SLAVES AND BIRDS AND ANIMALS

HIGH-KICKING BESSIE-JANE (Northwest Frontier of India)

This stone is erected in respectful memory of Bessie-Jane, one of the liveliest mules ever to make a British soldier resort to swearing. In her lifetime she kicked two colonels, two majors, two captains, three lieutenants, five sergeants, eleven corporals, eighteen privates and, alas, one live grenade. It may be truly said that she kicked her way through life into death.

BLACK BESS

Dick Turpin, was born at Hempstead, Essex, in 1705. He was 'successively and simultaneously' a butcher's apprentice, cattle-lifter, smuggler, house-breaker, highwayman and thief. To avoid the law, it is said that he rode non-stop from London to York, a distance of around 200 miles, in sixteen hours. His mare was to become famous as Black Bess, and the legend was immortalised in William Harrison Ainsworth's *Rookwood* (1834).

From the West was her dam; from the East her sire,
From the one came her swiftness; the other her fire,
No peer of the realm better blood can possess,
Than flows in the blood of my bonny Black Bess.

FROM HENBURY CHURCHYARD, BRISTOL

Here
Lieth the body of
SCIPIO AFRICANUS
Negro servant of the Rt Honourable
Charles William, Earl of Suffolk
and Bristol.
Who died ye 21 Dec, 1720.

TO A HORSE (Manchester, 30 September 1843)

> Fallen from his fellow's side,
> The steed beneath is lying;
> In harness here he died;
> His only fault was dying.

THE TOMB OF A FISH (Blockley, Gloucestershire)

> In the memory of the old fish,
> Under the soil the old fish do lie,
> Twenty year he lived and then did die.
> He was so tame you understand,
> He would come and eat out of your hand.
>   Died April the 20th, 1855.

ON A GOLDFINCH (Beauchamp Tower, Tower of London)

Buried 23 June 1794 by a fellow-prisoner. The reference in the first line is to the imprisonment of the English adventurer and writer Sir Walter Raleigh for treason: he was released in 1616.

> Where Raleigh pin'd within a prison's gloom
> I cheerful sung, nor murmur'd at my doom
> Where heroes bold, and patriots firm could dwell;
> A goldfinch in content, his note might swell,
> But death, more gentle than the law's decree,
> Hath paid my ransom from captivity.

> Full sixty years the angry Winters Wave
> Has thundering dash'd this bleak & barren Shore,
> Since SAMBO'S Head laid in this lonely GRAVE
> Lies still & ne'er will hear their turmoil more.

Full many a Sandbird chirps upon the Sod
And many a Moonlight Elfin round him trips
Full many a Summer's Sunbeam warms the Clod
And many a teeming Cloud upon him drips.

But still he sleeps — till the awakening Sounds
Of the Archangel's Trump new life impart
Then the GREAT JUDGE his Approbation sounds
Not on Man's COLOR but his WORTH OF HEART.

H. Bell del.
1796

ANIMAL, VEGETABLE OR MINERAL?

Once on the wall of the George Inn, Wanstead,
London; and erected by two workmen who were
fined one guinea for stealing a cherry pie!

In Memory of
ye Cherry Pey
As cost ½ a Guiney
ye 17 of July
That day we had good cheer
Hope to do so many a Year.

R.C.1752   D. Terry

WILLIAM HOGARTH'S EPITAPH FOR HIS PET BULLFINCH

Alas poor Dick!
1760
Aged eleven

Two cross-bones of birds, over these a heart and a
death's head.

AT SUNDERLAND POINT, LANCASTER

Thoughtless and irreverent people having damaged
and defaced the plate, this replica was affixed.

RESPECT THIS LONELY GRAVE
Here lies
POOR SAMBO
A faithful NEGRO
Who
(Attending his Master from the West Indies)
DIED on his Arrival at SUNDERLAND

From a garden formerly belonging to Lord Cobham, at Stowe, Buckinghamshire.

To the memory of
SIGNOR FIDO
An Italian of good Extraction
Who came to England,
Not to *bite* us, like most of his Countrymen,
But to gain an honest Livelyhood.
He *hunted* not after Fame.
Yet acquired it.
Regardless of the Praise of his Friends,
But most sensible of their Love.
Tho' he lived among the Great.
He neither learnt nor flatter'd any Vice.
He was no Bigot
Tho' he doubted of none of the Thirty-nine
Articles:
And if to follow Nature,
And to respect the Laws of Society,
Be Philosophy;
He was a perfect Philosopher,
A faithful Friend,
An agreeable Companion,
A loving husband;
And, tho' an Italian,
Was distinguished by a numerous Offspring:
All which he liv'd to see take good Courses.
In his old age he retir'd
To the house of a Clergyman in the Country,
Where he finished his earthly Race,
And died an Honour and Example to the
whole species.
Reader,
This stone is guiltless of Flattery!

GEMS OF WISDOM

OF PROPHECIES

When pictures look alive with movements free,
When ships, like fishes, swim below the sea,
When men, outstripping birds, can scan the sky,
Then half the world deep drenched in blood shall lie.

This, from Essex and *c* 1400, is the only example of a 'prophetic epitaph' in Britain, although there exists a stone at Clifton, Yorkshire, immortalising a prophetess:

> HERE LIES SHE THAT NEVER LY'D,
> WHOSE SKILL SO OFTEN HAS BEEN TRY'D,
> HER PROPHECIES SHALL STILL SURVIVE,
> AND EVER KEEP HER NAME ALIVE.

This stone was set up for Ursula Sontheil, known as 'Mother Shipton' (1488–1561). She wrote many verses which were deemed prophetic, including the following 'epitaph':

> The Crown then fits the White King's head,
> Who with the Lilies soon shall wed:
> Then shall a peasant's bloody knife
> Deprive a great man of his life.

There were those who interpreted the 'White King' as referring to Charles I, who was robed in white for his coronation. He married Henrietta Maria, sister to Henry IV of France, so that the 'Lilies' are the arms of France.

IN ST MICHAEL'S CHURCHYARD, DUMFRIES

In memory of J. M., died 31 August 1708, aged 50.

> If grace, good manners, gifts of mind,
> Yea where all moral virtues have combined,
> Compleat a man, behold beneath this stone,
> Here lyes interred, whom rich and poor bemoan,
> He run his race, abundant entrance got,
> His name is savori, and shall not rot.

In memory of B. C., died 5 December 1801, aged 64.

On what a slender thread hangs Everlasting things.

FROM TINWALD CHURCHYARD, DUMFRIESSHIRE

In memory of T. B., who died 1804.

> That truth how certain when this life is o'er,
> Man dies to live, and lives to die no more.

A SEPTUAGENARIAN'S ADVICE (Kirkmahoe churchyard, Dumfriesshire, 1700)

> Weep not for me who here do lye,
> Weep for your sins before you dye,
> For death is not to be lamented,
> But sin is still to be repented.

ON JOHN ORGONE AND HIS WIFE, ELLYNE (St Olave's Church, Hart Street, London, 1584)

> As I was, so be ye;
> As I am, you shall be:
> That I gave, that I have;
> That I spent, that I had,
> That I ende all my coste
> That I lefte, that I loste.

ROBERTUS OF DONCASTER

> How now, who is heare?
> I, Robin of Doncastere,
> And Margaret my feare.
> Quoth Robertus Byrks, who in this world did reign three-score years and seven, and yet lived not one.

IN CREDITON CHURCHYARD, DEVON

> Why do I live in life a thralle
> of joye and alle berefte?
> Their wings were growne
> to Heaven they're flowne,
> 'Cause I had none I'm lefte.

A time of death there is
  you know full well:
But when, or how 'twill come,
  no man can tell:
At midnight, morn, or noon:
  remember then,
Death is most certain, though
  uncertain when.

TWO FROM WETHERAL, CUMBRIA

In this vain world short was my stay,
And empty was my laughter.
I go before to clear the way,
And you'll come jogging after.

Here lieth the Body of Joseph Braddick, of this Parish, who Died the 27th Day of June, 1673, in the 40th year of his age.

Strong and at labour,
Suddenly he reels,
Death came behind him
And stroke up his heels;
Such sudden stroke
Surviving mortals bid ye
Stand on your watch
And to be also ready.

A DYER OF CLOTH (St Nicholas' Church, Yarmouth)

Here lies a man who first did dye,
When he was twenty-four,
And yet he lived to reach the age
Of Hoary hairs, fourscore.
But now he's gone, and certain 'tis
He'll not dye any more.

IT MUST COME (Melton Mowbray churchyard)

From the tomb of Mrs Stone.

Curious enough we all must say,
That what was stone should now be clay;
Most curious still, to owe we must,
That what was stone must soon be dust.

45

ADVICE (Chatham churchyard, Kent)

Weep not for him, the warmest tear that's shed
Falls unavailing o'er the unconscious dead;
Take the advice these friendly lines would give
Live not to drink, but only drink to live.

FROM THE NECROPOLIS, GLASGOW

Stranger as you pass o'er this grass;
Think seriously, with no humdrumming,
Prepare for death, for judgement's coming.

IN LEYLAND CHURCHYARD

Let the wind go free
Where'er thou be,
For twas the wind
That killed me.

JOHNNIE'S HOPE (Lincoln churchyard)

Here lies John Hyde;
He first liv'd, and then died;
He dyed to live, and liv'd to dye
And hopes to live eternally.

ON WOMEN

Censure not rashly,
Though nature's apt to halt,
No woman's born,
That dies without a fault.

ADMONISHMENT (Worstead churchyard, Norfolk)

These lines are not to praise the dead
But to admonish those by whom they're read:
Whatever his failings were, leave them alone,
And use thine utmost care to mend thine own.

FROM BROUGHTON, NORTHAMPTONSHIRE

Time was I stood where thou dost now,
And viewed the dead, as thou dost me;
Ere long thou'lt be as low as I,
And others stand and look on thee.

ON THE SOUTH WALL OF RUINED ELGIN CATHEDRAL,
MORAYSHIRE

The world is a city full of streets,
And death the mercat that all men meets,
If lyfe were a thing that monie could bye,
The poor could not live, and the rich would not die.

IN GRINDON CHURCH, NEAR LEEK, STAFFORDSHIRE

From a tomb near the chancel door.

Farewell, dear friends; to follow me prepare;
Also our loss we'd have you to beware,
And your own business mind. Let us alone,
For you have faults great plenty of your own.
Judge not of us, now we are in our graves
Lest ye be judg'd and awful sentence have;
For backbiters, railers, thieves, and liars,
Must torment have in everlasting fires.

THE MOURNFUL TRUTH

Death comes to all — none can resist his dart,
At his command the dearest friends must part;
A mournful widow, who this truth doth own,
In gratitude erects this humble stone.

FROM OTHER LANDS

France

Poor Charles!
His innocent pleasure was to row on the water
Alas!
He was the victim of this fatal desire,
Which conducted him to the tomb.
Reader! Consider that the water in which he was
drowned
Is the amassed tears of his relatives and friends.

FROM DIJON

Jean le Menestrier lieth here:
Lo: having number'd his seventieth year,
He tightens his stirrups, his spurs he plies,
And starts away for Paradise.

A TOMB IN THE VILLAGE OF AUTHIEUX, NEAR ROUEN

Look, man, before thee, how thy death hasteth;
Look, man, behind thee, how thy life wasteth —
Look on thy right side, how death thee desireth;
Look on thy left side, how sin thee beguileth —
Look, man, above thee, joys that will ever last.
Look, man, beneath thee, the pains without rest.

A 'SALT AND VINEGAR' EPITAPH FROM NANTES

Beneath this stone a quibbling lawyer lies
For sixty years who squeezed his neighbour's
purses;
If he can see you now, I'm sure he cries
That you have paid no fee to read these verses.

A PARIS BROTHEL-OWNER

He gladdened many hearts.

ANOTHER FROM NANTES

Dear friends and companions all
Pray warning take from me.
Don't venture on the ice too far
For 'twas the death of me.

THE MILLER OF TOULOUSE

Alas friend Pierre
His end was very sudden
As though a mandate came
Express from Heaven.
His foot did slip, and he did fall.
Help, help, he cried, and that was all.

THE TOMB OF AN ENGLISH MERCENARY AT LILLE

Oh Cruel Death: To make three meals in one.
To taste and taste till all was gone.
But know, thou Tyrant, when the trump shall call
He'll find his feet and stand when thou shall fall.

Apparently this soldier first lost a toe through gangrene, afterwards a leg, and then his life.

A GLUTTON OF NICE

This disease you'll never discover
I died from eating melon.
Be careful then all those who feed
For I was ere a glutton.

Germany

IN LÜNEBURG, HANOVER

The epitaph to a pig on the Town Hall.

Passer-by, contemplate here the mortal remains of
the pig
which acquired for itself imperishable glory by the
discovery of the salt springs of Lüneburg.

FROM DORTMUND CEMETERY, WESTPHALIA

Heinrich Bruggeman heiss ich,
Nach dem Himmel reise ich,
Will mal seh'n Jesus macht,
Liebe Bruder, gute nacht.

A BACHELOR FROM BERLIN

At threescore winters' end I died,
A cheerless being, sole and sad,
The nuptial knot I never tied —
And wish my father never had.

A COMFORTABLE LAIR AT OBERWESSEL

Heinrich Muller's best bedroom.

Italy

FROM THE CATACOMBS, ROME

HIC VERUS QUI SEMPER VERA LOCUTUS

(Here lies Verus [Truth], who always spoke
truly.)

THE TOMB OF WICKED CHLOË

IN SCRIPSIT TUMULIS SEPTEM SCELERATA
VIRORUM SE FECISSE
CHLOË, QUID POTE SIMPLICIUS

(Wicked Chloë inscribed on the tombs of her seven
husbands 'I did this').

This Latin construction *Chloë fecit*, can mean either
'built this tomb' or 'caused the death of'.

50

Here lies one whose name is writ in water.

FROM FLORENCE

Here lies SALVINO ARMOLO D'ARMATI,
of Florence,
the inventor of spectacles.
May God pardon his sins!
The year 1318.

Netherlands

A SENIOR CITIZEN OF GRONINGEN

Do not mock an old woman
No one knows his fate
From old age and death God alone is free
All other things change with time
And that means you.

Australia

LITTLE NELL

God took our flower — our little Nell,
He thought He too would like a smell.

A MAN WHO DROVE AN ARMOURED TRAIN AT THE
KIMBERLEY GOLDFIELD

No more will he stand on the footplate,
No more will he steam into town.
He has shut off his steam for ever,
And gone to pick up his crown.

THE DOWNS FROM SOUTH AUSTRALIA

In memory of
Eileen, Ida, Ben and Bob
DOWN.

Greece

Sardanapalus, son of Anacyndaraxes, caused the towns of Auchiales and Tarsus to be built in a single day. Pass on stranger. Eat, drink, and enjoy yourself, for naught else is worth a fillip.

India

A MISSIONARY

Sacred to the Memory of
The Rev — —
Who, after twenty years' unremitting labour
as a Missionary
Was accidentally shot by his native bearer.
'WELL DONE THOU GOOD AND FAITHFUL SERVANT'
Matthew 25:21.

TOMBSTONE FROM MIDNAPORE, WEST BENGAL

Stop, readers, and lament the loss of a departed
beauty,
for here are laid at rest the earthly relicks of
MRS SUSANNA BIRD
who bade a long adieu to
a most affectionate husband and three loved
pledges of their union on the 10th September,
1784,
aged twenty-four years.

The bird confined within this cage of gloom.
Tho' faded her fine tints, her youthful bloom.
Tho' no soft note drop from her syren's tongue,
By sleep refresh'd more beauteous gay and young.
Will rise from earth, her seraph's wings display,
And chaunt her anthems to the God of day.

FOR TINKER, TAILOR,
SOLDIER AND SAILOR

Here lies honest William, a good natured fellow
Who did far too often get rubicund mellow.
Body-coachman was he to an eminent brewer —
No better e'er sat on a box to be sure.
His coach was kept clean, and no mothers or nurses
Took that care of their babies as he took of his
    horses.
He had these — ay, and fifty good qualities more,
But the business of tippling could ne'er be got o'er:
So his master effectually mended the matter,
By hiring a man who drank nothing but water.
'Now William', says he, 'you see the plain case,
If you drink as he does then you'll keep your place'.
'Drink water!' quoth William, 'I'd far sooner die'.
And now with his ancestors William do lie.

THOMAS THE WIGMAKER, d 1735, AND HIS WIFE (St
Michael's churchyard, Dumfries)

> Two lovers true for ten years' space absented,
> By stormy seas, and wars, yet liv'd contented,
> We met for eighteen years, and married were.
> God smil'd on us, our wind bleue always fair,
> We're ancor'd here, waiting our Master's call,
> Expecting with Him, joys perpetuall.

THE TOWN DRUMMER (Langholm churchyard,
Selkirkshire)

> Interred here, Archibald Beattie, town
> drummer, who for more than half a century
> kept up the ancient and annual custom of
> proclaiming the Langholm Fair at the Cross
> when riding the common granted to the
> town, and pointing out to the inhabitants
> thereof the various boundaries of those

rights which descended from their ancestors to posterity. He died in 1823, aged 90 years. The managers of the Common-Riding for the year 1829 have caused his name to be here inscribed, as a tribute of respect due to his memory.

FOR A DECEASED RAILWAY GUARD (Crewe)

Short was his passage through this earthly vale,
By railway lines where mortals used to wend;
But now he travels by way of heaven's rail,
As soon again to reach his journey's end.

A DOCTOR OF THEOLOGY (Salendine Nook Baptist Chapel, Huddersfield, West Yorkshire)

You tell us, Doctor, 'tis a sin to steal;
We to your practice from your text appeal.
You steal a sermon, steal a nap; and pray
From dull companions don't you steal away.

THE WOOL DRESSER OF DUNDEE

Here lie the banes o'Tammas Messer
Of tarry woo he was a dresser:
He had some faults and mony merits
And died o'drinking ardent spirits.

THE DOCTOR'S EPITAPH (Castleton churchyard, Roxburghshire)

John Armstrong, M.D., born 1709, died 1779.
If yet thy shade delights to hover near
The holy ground, where oft thy sire hath taught,
And where our fathers fondly flocked to hear;
Accept the offering which their sons have brought.
Proud of the muse, which gave to classic fame,
Our vale and stream, to song before unknown,
We raise this stone to bear thy deathless name
And tell the world that Armstrong was our own,
To learning worth and genius, such as thine,
How vain the tribute monuments can pay!
Thy name immortal with thy works shall shine,
And live where frailer marbles shall decay.

THE CARRIER'S STORY (Kilbride churchyard)

Here lye the banes of Thamas Tyre,
Wha lang had trudged through dub and mire,
In carrying bundles and sic like,
His task performing wi' sma' fyke.
To deal in snuff he aye was free,
And served his friends for little fee,
His life obscure was naething new,
Yet we must own his faults were few.
Although at Yule he sipped a drap,
And in the kirk whiles took a nap,
True to his work in every case
Tam scorned to cheat for lucre base;
Now he has gone to taste the fare
Which only honest men will share.

ON A CRICKETER (Salisbury)

I bowl'd, I struck, I caught, I stopp'd,
  Sure life's a game of cricket;
I block'd with care, with caution popp'd
  Yet Death has hit my wicket.

THE SWEET SMELLING PRIEST (Winchester College, 1541)

> Beneath this stone lies shut up in the dark,
> A fellow and a priest, yclep'd JOHN CLARK
> With earthly rose-water he did delight ye,
> But now he deals in heavenly *aqua vitae*.

AT THE TOP OF A STAINED GLASS WINDOW IN A SUSSEX CHURCH

> To the Glory of God

and, set below:

> And in memory of his Grandfather.

THE HAMPSHIRE GRENADIER (Winchester Cathedral)

> In memory of
> THOMAS THATCHER
> A grenadier in the North Regt of Hants Militia, who died of a violent fever contracted by drinking small beer when hot, the 12th of May 1764. Aged 26 years. In grateful remembrance of whose universal good will towards his comrades, this stone is placed here at their expence as a small testimony of their regard and concern.

> Here sleeps in peace a Hampshire Grenadier,
> Who caught his death by drinking cold small beer;
> Soldiers, be wise from his untimely fall,
> And when you're hot drink strong, or none at all.

AN ORGANIST (Wakefield, West Yorkshire, Parish Church)

> In memory of
> HENRY CLEMETSHAW
> upwards of fifty years organist
> of this church, who died, May 7, 1821
> aged 86 years.

> Now like an organ, robb'd of pipes and breath,
> Its keys and stops are useless made by death.
> Tho mute re-built by more than mortal aid,
> This instrument, new voiced, and tuned, shall raise,
> To God, its builder, hymns of endless praise.

THE PEDLAR'S EPITAPH (Troutbeck, Cumbria)

If Bowness village you should know,
There may you hear my fyles to go,
Pins and needles, sirs, who buyes 'em,
Hard and sharp, whoever tryes 'em,
Toys and rattles to still babyes,
Temple wires, that's fit for ladyes.
Come and buy, if you'll have any,
I wod fain draw the packing penny.
Whilst the pedlar thus doth bawle,
And his wares for sale doth call,
Death passed by like one unknown,
Commands him pack — his market's done.

IN MEMORY OF WILLIAM RICHARD PHELPS, LATE
BOATSWAIN OF HMS INVINCIBLE

He accompanied Lord Anson on his cruise round the
world, and died 21 April 1789.

When I was like you,
For years, not a few,
On the ocean I toil'd,
On the line I have broil'd,
In Greenland I've shiver'd,
Now from hardships deliver'd,
Capsized by old Death
I surrender'd my breath,
And now I lie snug
As a bug in a rug.

SMITH, THE HABERDASHER (from a lost cemetery in
London)

Here lies John Smith, sometime Hosier and
    Haberdasher in this Town.
He left his hose, his Anna and his love,
To sing Hosanna in the realms above.

ON AN OLD SOLDIER'S GRAVE

God and our soldier we alike adore,
Just at the brink of danger, not before:
After the battle they're alike requited,
God is forbidden and the soldier slighted.

LINES ON A WAGGONER'S TOMB (Bisbrooke church-yard, Leicestershire)

Here lies the body of Nathaniel Clarke,
Who never did no harm in the light, nor in the dark,
But in his blessed horses, taking great delight,
And often travelled with them by day and night.

LINES ON A SMUGGLER

> Here I lies,
> Killed by the X.I.S.

THE ZEALOUS LOCKSMITH

> A zealous locksmith dy'd of late,
> And did arrive at Heaven's gate,
> He stood without and would not knock,
> Because he meant to pick the lock.

THE MAJOR OF HIGH WYCOMBE

Here lies removed from mundane scenes,
A major of the King's Marines,
Under arrest in narrow borders,
He rises not till further orders.

PEPPER'S GRAVE (St John's Church, Stamford)

On William Pepper,
Tho' hot my name, yet mild my nature,
I bore goodwill to every creature,
I brewed good ale, and sold it too,
And unto each I gave his due.

THE ROADMENDER (St Edith's churchyard, Eaton-under-Heywood, Salop)

Thomas Corfield, the author and Sole cause of
Mending the roads in his (bad) very bad neighbour-
hood.

CRUMMY ABERCROMBIE OF THE PENNY WHISTLE (Dumfries)

Here Crummy lies, enclosed in wood,
Full six feet one and better,
When tyrant death grim o'er him stood,
He faced him like a hatter.
Now lies he low without a boot,
Free from this world of bustle,
And silent now is Crummy's flute,
And awful dry his whustle.

A PAUPER'S GRAVE

Poorly lived
And poorly died,
Poorly Buried,
And no one cried.

A SEXTON'S STORY

Hurra! my brave boys,
Let's rejoice at his fall!
For if he had lived,
He had buried us all.

THE BLACKSMITH'S EPITAPH

This epitaph, written by the poet William Hayley (1745—1820), has proved a favourite with blacksmiths. Among other places it appears in the churchyards of Rochdale, Bothwell, Feltham and Westham.

> My sledge and hammer lie declined,
> My bellows-pipes have lost their wind,
> My fire's extinct, my forge decay'd,
> My vice is in the dust now laid;
> My coal is spent, my iron's gone,
> My nails are drove, my work is done,
> My fire-dried corpse here lies at rest,
> My soul, smoke-like, soars to be blest.

JOSEPH BLACKETT, POET AND SHOEMAKER (Seaham, County Durham)

Written by Lord Byron

> OBIT 1810
> Stranger! behold interr'd together
> The *souls* of learning and of leather.
> Poor Joe is gone, but left his *awl* —
> You'll find his relics in a *stall.*
> His work was neat, and often found
> Well-stitched and with morocco bound,
> Tread lightly — where the bard is laid
> He cannot mend the shoe he made;
> Yet he is happy as his *sole.*
> But still to business he held fast,
> And struck to Phoebus to the last.
> Then who shall say so good a fellow
> Was only leather and prunella?
> For character — he did not lack it,
> And if he did — 'twere shame to *Black-it*!

THE MILKMAN (Earls Barton, Northamptonshire)

> A milkman's tomb.
> Milk and water sold I ever,
> Weight and measure, gave I
>   never,
> So, to the devil I must go,
> Woe, woe, woe, woe.

THE WATCHMAKER (Bolsover, Derbyshire)

> Here lieth, in a horizontal position,
> The outsize case of THOMAS HINDE,
> Clock and Watchmaker.

Who departed this life, wound up in hope of being taken in hand by his Maker, and being thoroughly cleaned, repaired and set a-going in the world to come. On the 15th day of August 1836.

FROM ST DUNSTAN'S CHURCHYARD, STEPNEY

> Here lies the body of Daniel Saul,
> Spittlefield's weaver and that's all.

THE TOMB OF A SAILOR AND HIS WIFE (Cathedral cemetery, St Andrews)

> He we lie
> In horizontal position,
> Like a ship laid up
> Stript of her mast and riggin'.

THE PORTSMOUTH CARPENTER

Here lies JEMMY LITTLE, a carpenter industrious,
A very good-natured man, but somewhat
   blusterous.
When that his little wife his authority withstood,
He took a little stick and bang'd her as he would.
His wife, now left alone, her loss does so deplore,
She wishes JEMMY back to bang her a little more;
For now he's dead and gone this fault appears so
   small,
A little thing would make her think it was no fault
   at all.

ADAMS, THE CARRIER (Southwell churchyard, Nottinghamshire)

JOHN ADAMS lies here, of the parish of Southwell,
A carrier who carried his can to his mouth well;
He carried it much and he carried it fast,
He could carry no more — so was carried at last;
For the liquor, being too much for one,
He could carry off — so he's now carri-on.

A FAVOURITE MISCELLANY

THE DUNMORE GROCER (County Waterford)

> Here lie the remains of JOHN HALL, grocer,
> The world is not worth a fig, and
> I have good raisins for saying so.

A SMALL-TIME SHOPKEEPER (Wigtown churchyard)

> Here lies John Taggart, of honest fame,
> Of stature low, and a leg lame;
> Content he was with portion small,
> Kept a shop in Wigtown, and that's all.

FROM UPTON-ON-SEVERN CHURCHYARD

> Beneath this stone in hopes of Zion,
> Doth lie the landlord of the Lion;
> His son keeps on the business still,
> Resigned upon the heavenly will.

ON A LONDON BOOKSELLER

> Here lies poor NED PARDON, from misery freed,
> Who long was a bookseller's hack;
> He led such a damnable life in this world,
> I don't think he'll ever come back.

ON HUSBAND AND WIFE

> Here lies the body of JAMES ROBERTSON and RUTH his
> wife.
> 'Their warfare is accomplished.'

A QUICK DEMISE

> Sudden and unexpected was the end,
> Of our esteemed and beloved friend,
> He gave to all his friends a sudden shock,
> By one day falling into Sunderland dock.

MARTHA SNELL AND ANN MANN

Poor Martha Snell! her's gone away,
Her would if her could, but her couldn't stay;
Her'd two sore legs and a baddish cough,
But her legs it was as carried her off.

Here lies Ann Mann;
She lived an old Maid,
And she died an old Mann.

TO AN ANGLER

He angled many a purling brook,
But lacked the angler's skill:
He lied about the fish he took,
And here he's lying still.

TOO MUCH AND TOO LATE

Here lies I and my three daughters,
Killed by drinking Cheltenham waters,
If we'd kept to Epsom Salts,
We wouldn't be lying in these 'ere vaults.

Here lies the Mother of Twenty-eight,
It might have been more, but now it's too late.

IN A FEW WORDS

Here lies the wife of Simon Stokes.
Who lived and died like other folks.

FROM GUNWALLOW CHURCHYARD, NEAR HELSTON, CORNWALL

Shall weee all die?
Weee shall die all.
All die shall weee?
Die all weee shall.

FROM WOOD TO BUN

Here lies John Bun,
He was killed by a gun.
His name was not Bun but Wood,
But Wood would not rhyme with Gun,
     but Bun would.

JOHN BROWN, THE DENTIST

Stranger! Approach this spot with gravity!
John Brown is filling his last cavity.

OLD JOHN HILDIBRODD

Here lies old John Hildibrodd,
Have mercy on him, Good God,
As he would if he was God,
And Thou wer't old John Hildibrodd.